CONTENTS

Cover Photo: Paul D'Innocenzo

ISBN 0-7935-9755-2

HAL•LEONARD® CORPORATION

7777 W. BLUEMOUND RD. P.O. BOX 13819 MILWAUKEE, WI 53213

Visit Hal Leonard Online at
www.halleonard.com

Michael Brecker—Biography

Equally at ease – and in demand – in the jazz and pop idioms, seven-time Grammy Award-winning tenor saxophonist and composer Michael Brecker is a major figure in contemporary instrumental music. Brecker is the first recording artist ever to win Grammys for both Best Jazz Instrumental Performance and Best Jazz Instrumental Solo two years in a row.

Born in Philadelphia, Pennsylvania on March 29, 1949, Brecker was exposed to jazz as far back as he can remember. His attorney dad was also a semi-professional jazz pianist. In addition to hearing his older brother Randy practicing trumpet, Michael remembers listening to records by Dave Brubeck and Clifford Brown, and seeing Miles Davis, Thelonious Monk, Duke Ellington and many other greats in person while still a child. It was John Coltrane, however, who inspired Brecker to pursue music as a career.

After early studies on the clarinet and alto sax, Brecker began playing tenor sax in high school. In 1966, he followed Randy to the University of Indiana at Bloomington, opting for a major in fine arts rather than music.

In 1968, Brecker moved to New York, exhilarated by the thriving, divergent music scene there. In the late '60s he became a founding member of the ground-breaking jazz-rock ensemble Dreams. This group was one of the first bands to fuse a horn section (featuring Michael, Randy, and trombonist Barry Rogers) on top of rock rhythms (the rhythm section featured guitarist John Abercrombie, drummer Billy Cobham, pianist Don Grolnick and bassist Will Lee).

In 1973, Brecker switched modes and launched into the traditional jazz scene. He joined Randy as the front line of pianist Horace Silver's quintet, followed by five years helming the Brecker Brothers, recording six albums and earning seven Grammy nominations along the way. During this time, Michael and Randy opened the legendary jazz club Seventh Avenue South. It was there that the band Steps Ahead evolved through late-night jamming between Michael, Don Grolnick, vibraharpist Mike Mainieri, drummer Steve Gadd, and bassist Eddie Gomez.

By the mid '70s Brecker was recording and performing with the most respected and renowned names in jazz, including Chet Baker, George Benson, Dave Brubeck, Don Cherry, Chick Corea, Herbie Hancock, Freddie Hubbard, Quincy Jones, Pat Metheny, Charles Mingus, Jaco Pastorius, Horace Silver and Tony Williams. He also played with an exhaustive list of pop icons including John Lennon, Bruce Springsteen, Frank Zappa, Frank Sinatra and many others.

In 1987, Michael's self-titled solo debut was voted Jazz Album of the Year by *Downbeat* and *Jazziz* magazines. His next album, *Don't Try This at Home*, won a Grammy. His third solo album, *Now You See It, Now You Don't*, was followed by a year and a half tour and a recording with Paul Simon, after which the Brecker Brothers reunited for two albums. 1994's *Out of the Loop* earned Michael another two Grammys, including Best Instrumental Composition for his "African Skies." Selections from this album and its predecessor, *Return of the Brecker Brothers*, are now available on the *Brecker Brothers' Priceless Jazz* release on GRP.

Brecker's fourth solo album, *Tales from the Hudson* (1996) reunited Michael with Pat Metheny and Jack DeJohnette, both of whom appeared on his acclaimed solo debut. *Tales* won two more Grammy awards and was named Album of the Year in a number of jazz magazines worldwide. 1997 saw Brecker named Best Jazz Soloist of the Year by *Jazz Life*, and Jazz Man of the Year by *Swing Journal*. In 1998, Impulse released *Two Blocks from the Edge* which was later voted #3 on the Gavin Report's list of Jazz Top 100 Albums for that year.

Michael brings the millenium to a close with the release of his sixth solo album, entitled (appropriately!) *Time Is of the Essence*, featuring Elvin Jones, Pat Metheny, Larry Goldings, Jeff "Tain" Watts and Bill Stewart, with concerts to continue in clubs and concert halls around the world.

Carl Coan—Biography

Carl Coan attended Berklee College of Music and received his Masters Degree in saxophone performance from Indiana University, South Bend. He performs and teaches in the Chicago area. Questions and comments can be sent to carlcoan@yahoo.com. Thanks to Robert Baglione for his help with the chord changes.

Michael Brecker—Discography

Albums issued under Michael Brecker's name

MICHAEL BRECKER – IMPULSE MCAD-5980
DON'T TRY THIS AT HOME – IMPULSE MCAD-42229
NOW YOU SEE IT…NOW YOU DON'T – GRD-9622
TALES FROM THE HUDSON – IMPULSE IMPD-191
TWO BLOCKS FROM THE EDGE – IMPULSE IMPD-260
TIME IS OF THE ESSENCE – VERVE 314 547 844-2

Additional albums

OUT OF THE LOOP – THE BRECKER BROTHERS – GRD-9784
(AFRICAN SKIES is also available on
The Brecker Bros. Priceless Jazz – GRD-9948)
LIVE IN TOKYO 1986 – STEPS AHEAD – NYC-6006
INFINITY – McCOY TYNER – IMPULSE IMPD-171

Notation Guide
Saxophone

♪	grace note	L.D.	lip down from previous note
♪	long grace note	L.D.^{1}	finger note one half step higher and lip down
♪	ghost note	L.D.^{2}	finger note two half steps higher and lip down
♭ ♯	note is slightly flat or sharp	L.D.^{3}	finger note three half steps higher and lip down
+	alternate fingering	R	slightly rush
⊕	special alternate fingering	D	slightly delay
o	overtone on given lower note	h.t.	half tongue
Ⓜ	multiphonic	d.t.	double tongue
(or)	bend note up or down using jaw	01	overtone on low B♭
sb	slow bend	02	overtone on low B
∅	cracked note (note also sounds *8vb*)	03	overtone on low C
Ⓢ	split tone altissimo note	04	overtone on low C♯
B	breath attack	05	overtone on low D
Ⓥ	vocalized altissimo note (à la Trane)	06	overtone on low E♭
*	Freak out (rapidly move fingers up and down keys while getting pitch using jaw)		

EWI

written in B♭ and sounds 1 octave higher than tenor

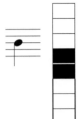 Set pitch bend for one whole step

 the B is fingered A with the pitchbend up

 bend note from one whole step away

 bend note from 1 half step away

 the A is fingered B with the pitchbend down

 ghost note

 grace note

 long grace note

 bend note using thumb

*   bite on mouthpiece as you end note

 note is slightly flat or sharp

Suggested Alternative Fingerings

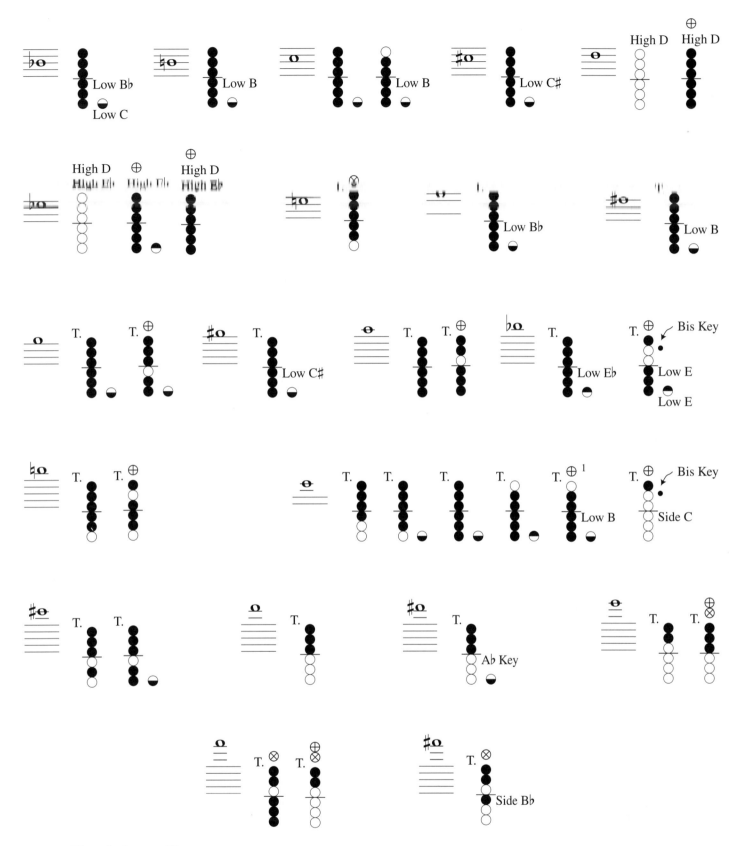

T. Thumb Octave Key

⊗ Front F Key

⊕ Special Alternate Fingering

Suggested Altissimo Fingerings

All fingerings can be used as split tones and vocalized notes

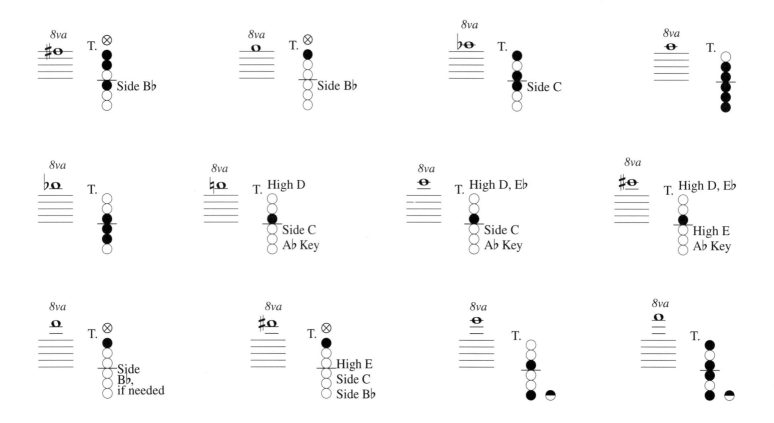

(S) split tones: more than one pitch; top given note will sound strongest

(V) vocalized notes: singing, growling or humming with note (à la John Coltrane)

Suggested Multiphonics

(M) multiphonics: more than one equal sounding pitch

Overtones

All notes marked as an overtone have at least a hint of a lower harmonic.

Overtone 1

Overtone 2

Overtone 3

Overtone 4

sounds as F♯ on Tenor; can also sound as High F when played flat

Overtone 5

Overtone 6

African Skies

from *Out of the Loop*

By Michael Brecker

African Skies
from *Tales from the Hudson*
By Michael Brecker

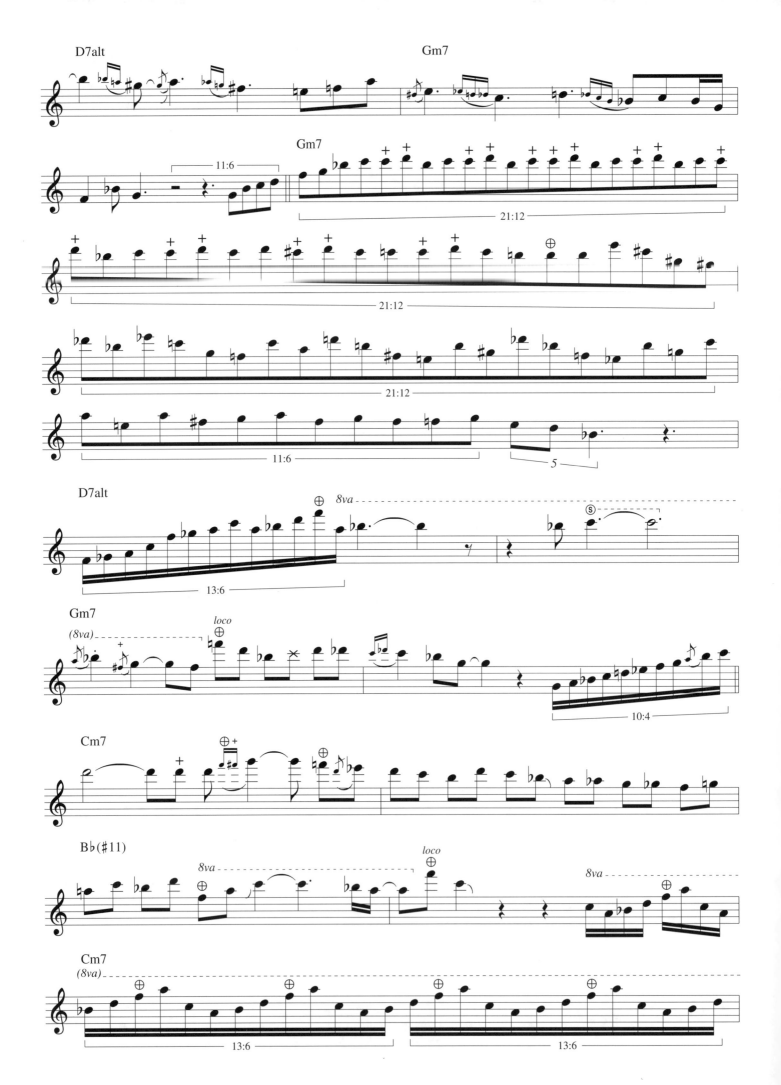

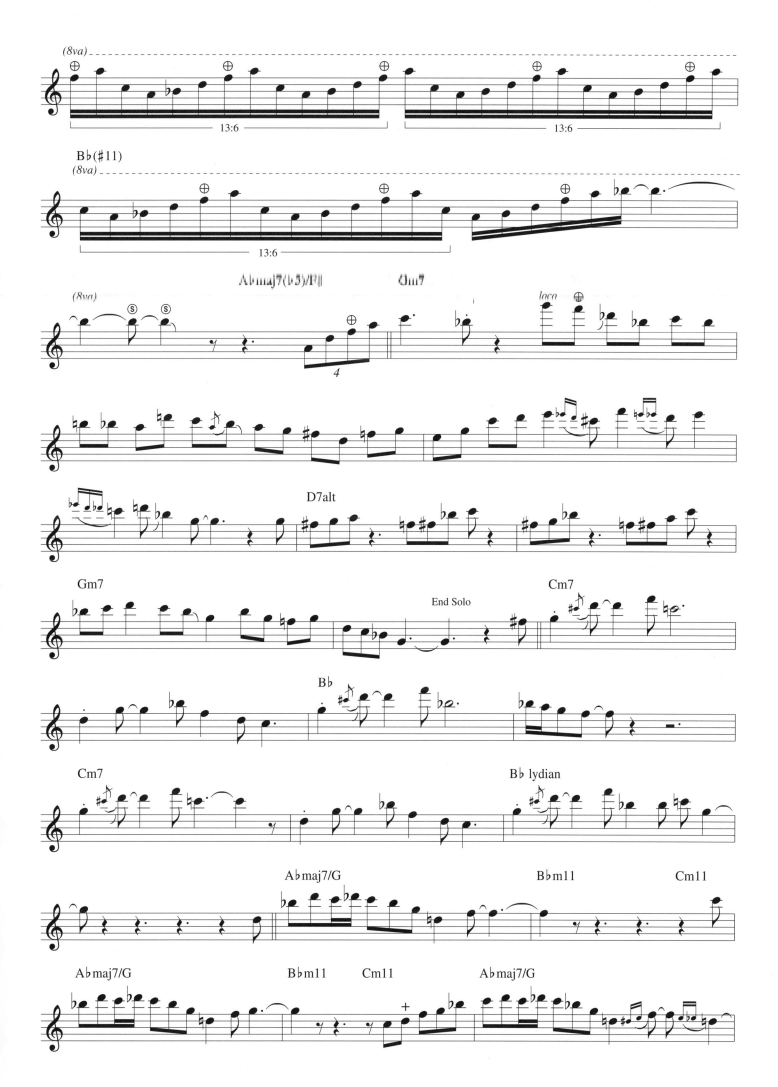

* = finger as high B, A♭, G♭, and F

Beirut

from *Live in Tokyo*

By Michael Brecker, Peter Erskine, Chuck Loeb, Mike Mainieri and Victor Bailey

EWI Solo

* = bite on mouthpiece as you end note

Cabin Fever

from *Tales from the Hudson*

By Michael Brecker

* = Finger theses notes as altis. B♭ and lip up.

Beau Rivage

from *Tales from the Hudson*

By Michael Brecker

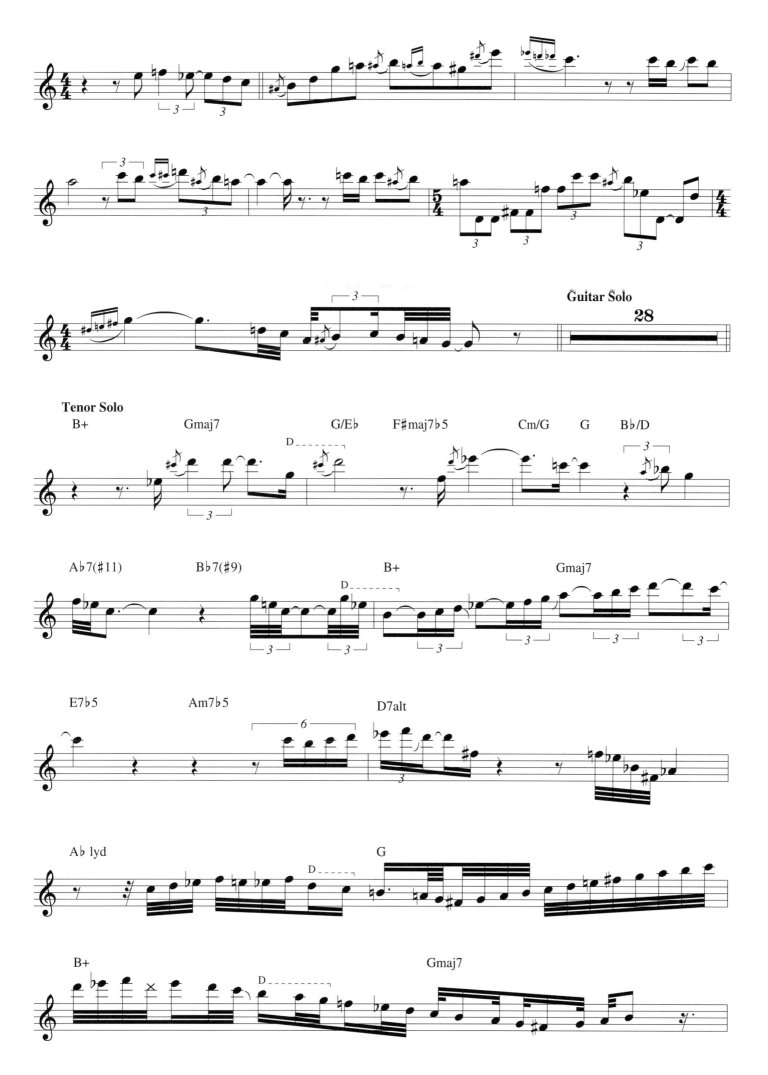

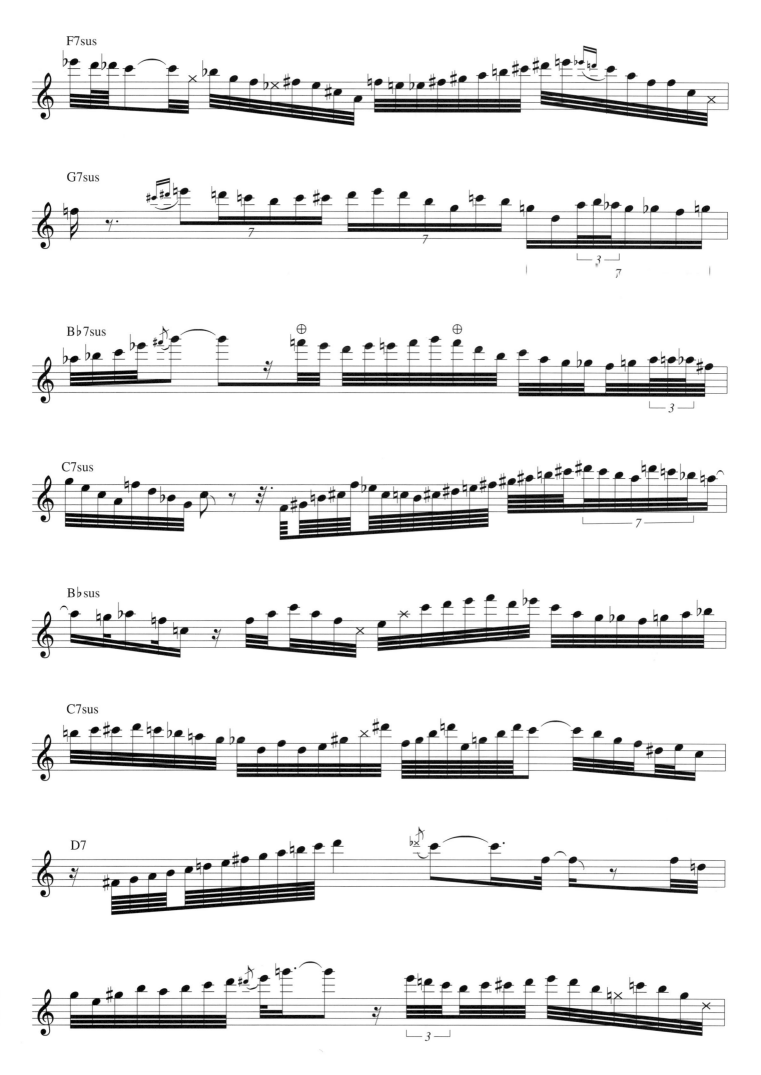

Delta City Blues

from *Two Blocks from the Edge*

By Michael Brecker

Rhumba with Band

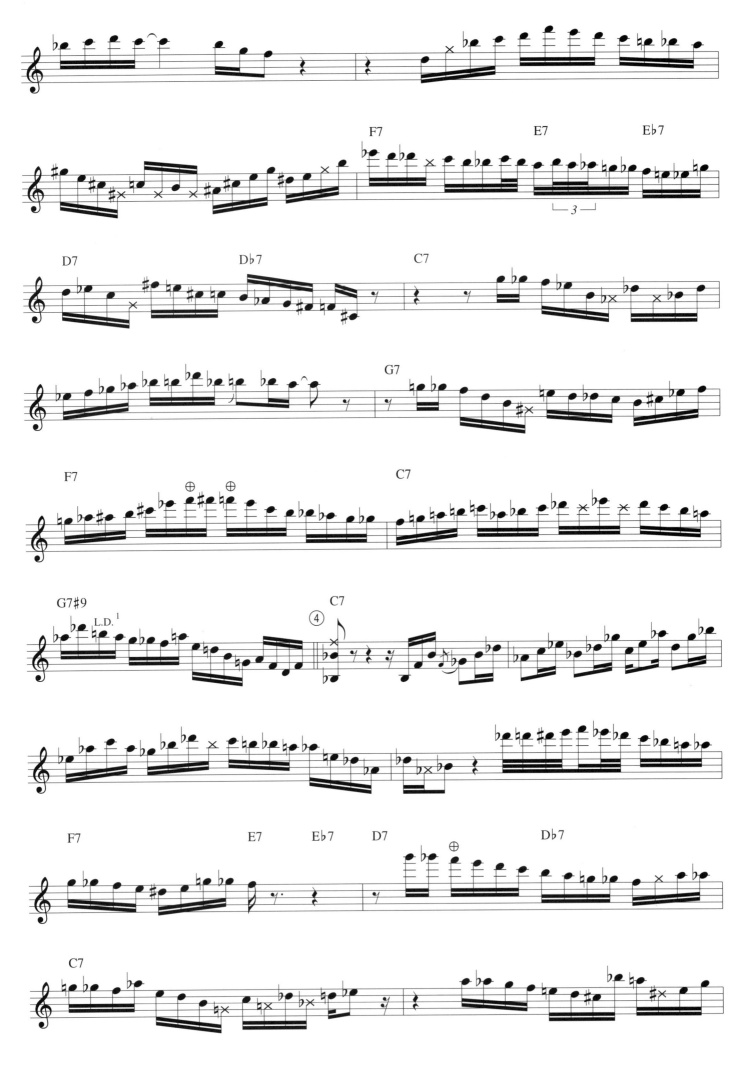

El Niño

from *Two Blocks from the Edge*
By Joey Calderazzo

Impressions

from McCoy Tyner, *Infinity*
By John Coltrane

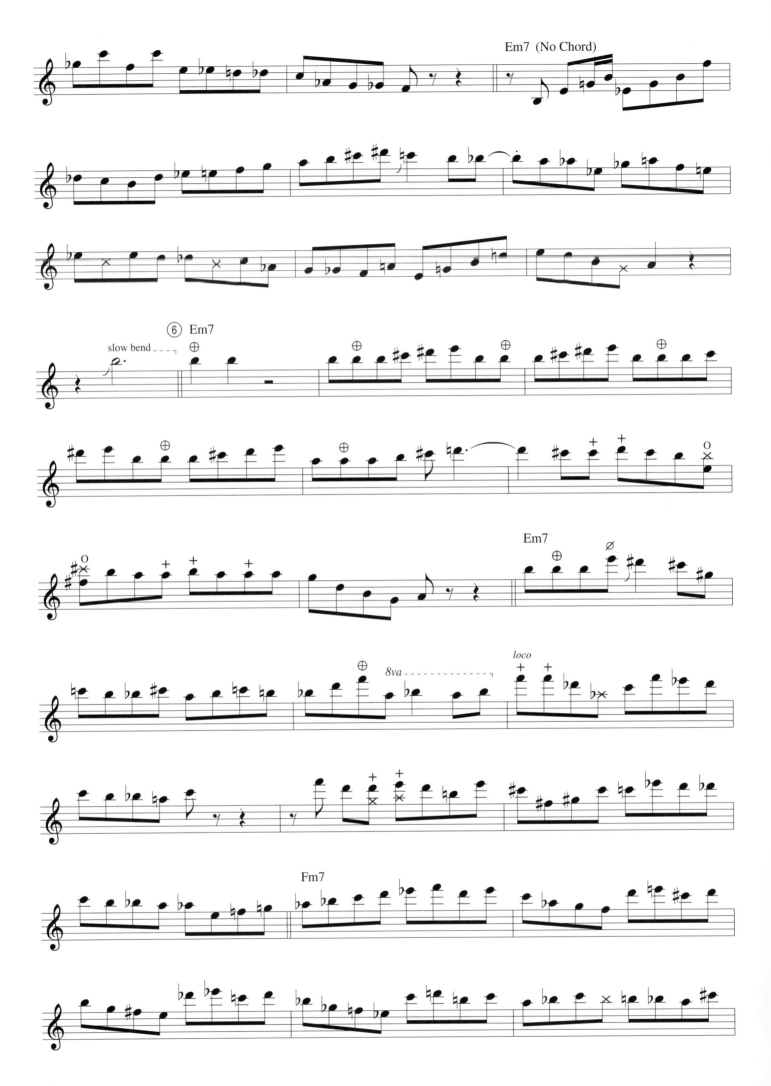

How Long 'til the Sun

from *Two Blocks from the Edge*

By Michael Brecker

Madame Toulouse

from *Two Blocks from the Edge*

By Michael Brecker

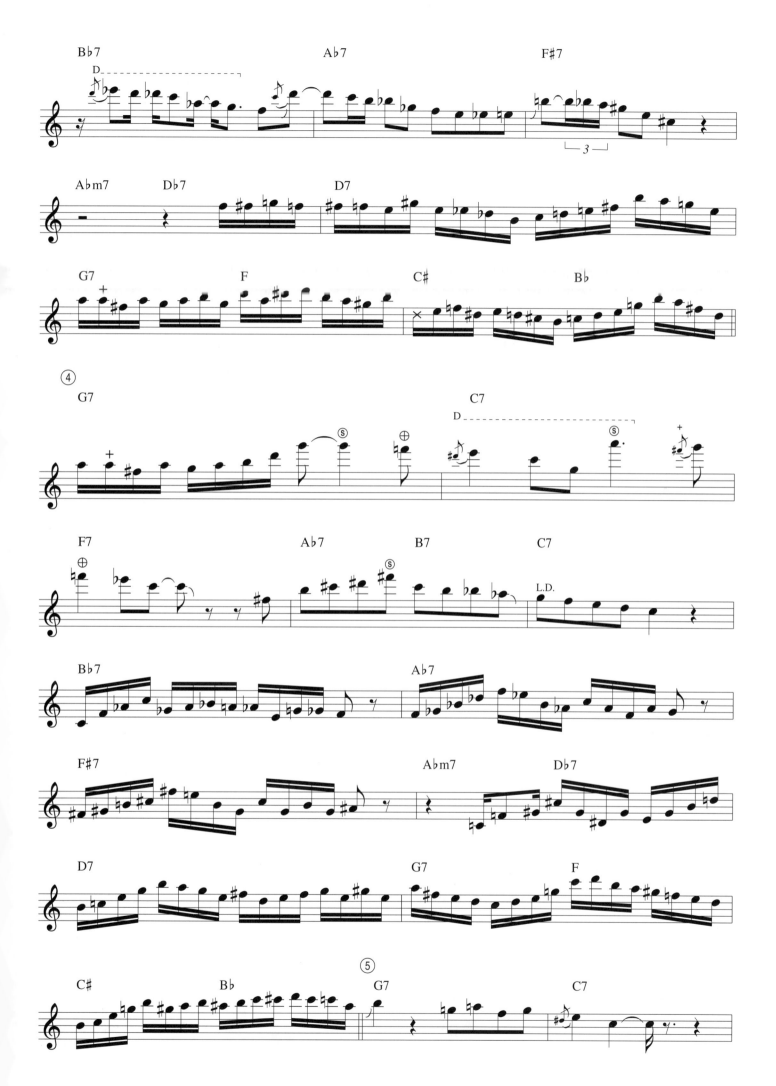

Naked Soul

from *Tales from the Hudson*

By Michael Brecker

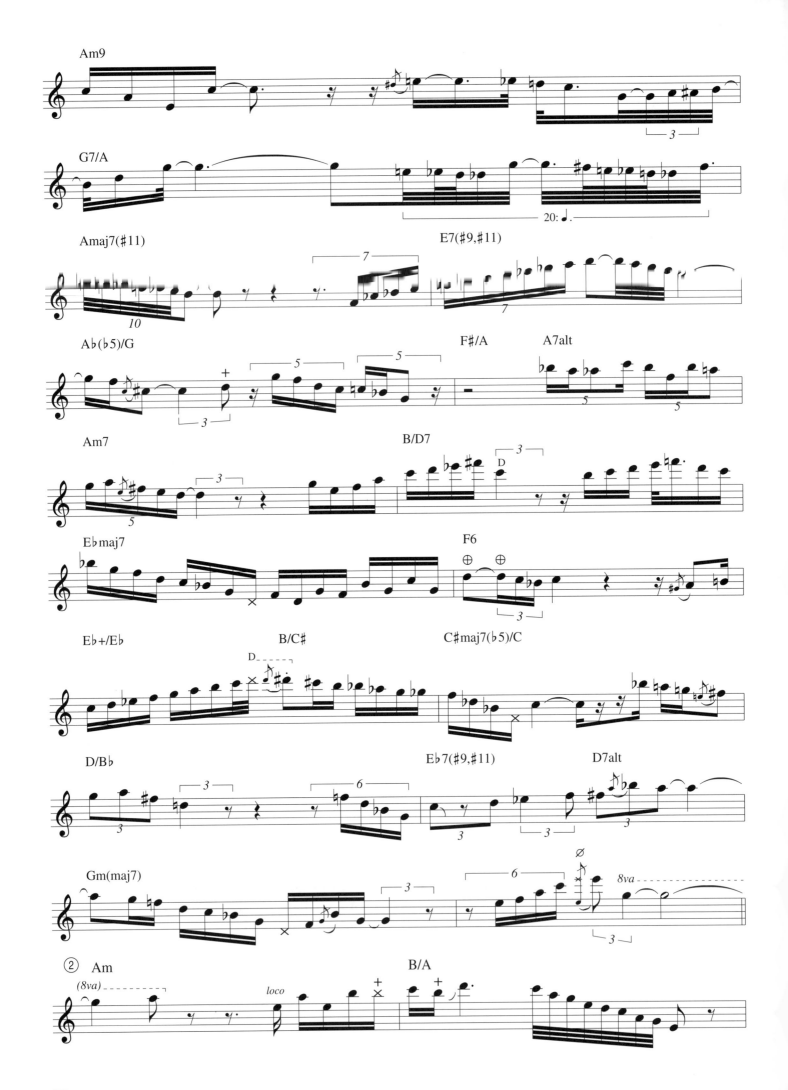

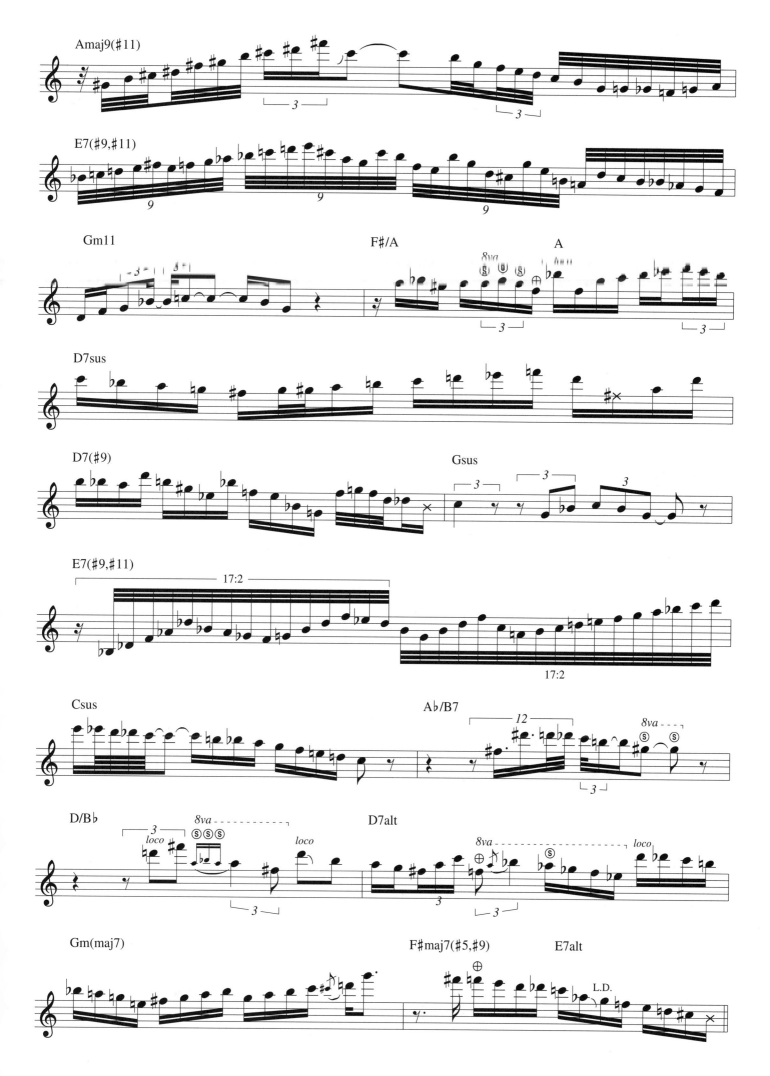

* = finger as altis. G

Slings & Arrows

from *Tales from the Hudson*

By Michael Brecker

Tenor Solo

Piano Solo

Syzygy

from *Michael Brecker*

By Michael Brecker

*h.t. = half tongue

Piano Solo   **Soli with EWI**
G pedal
out

Sumo

from *Live in Tokyo 1986*

By Michael Brecker

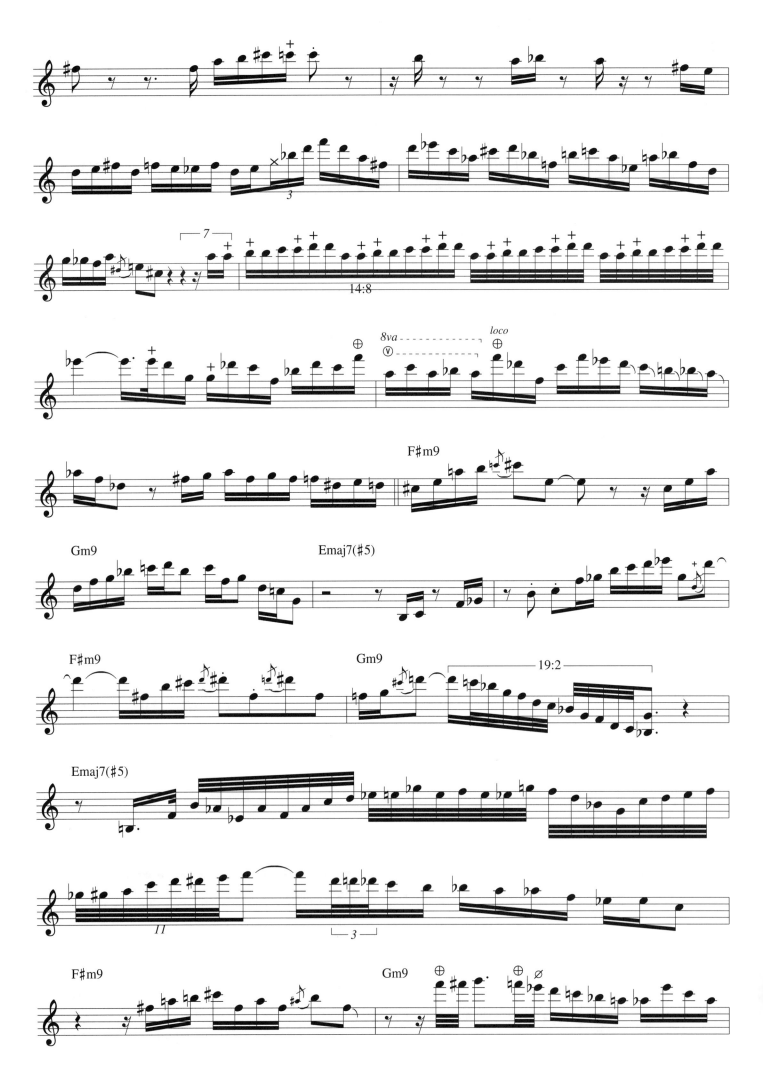

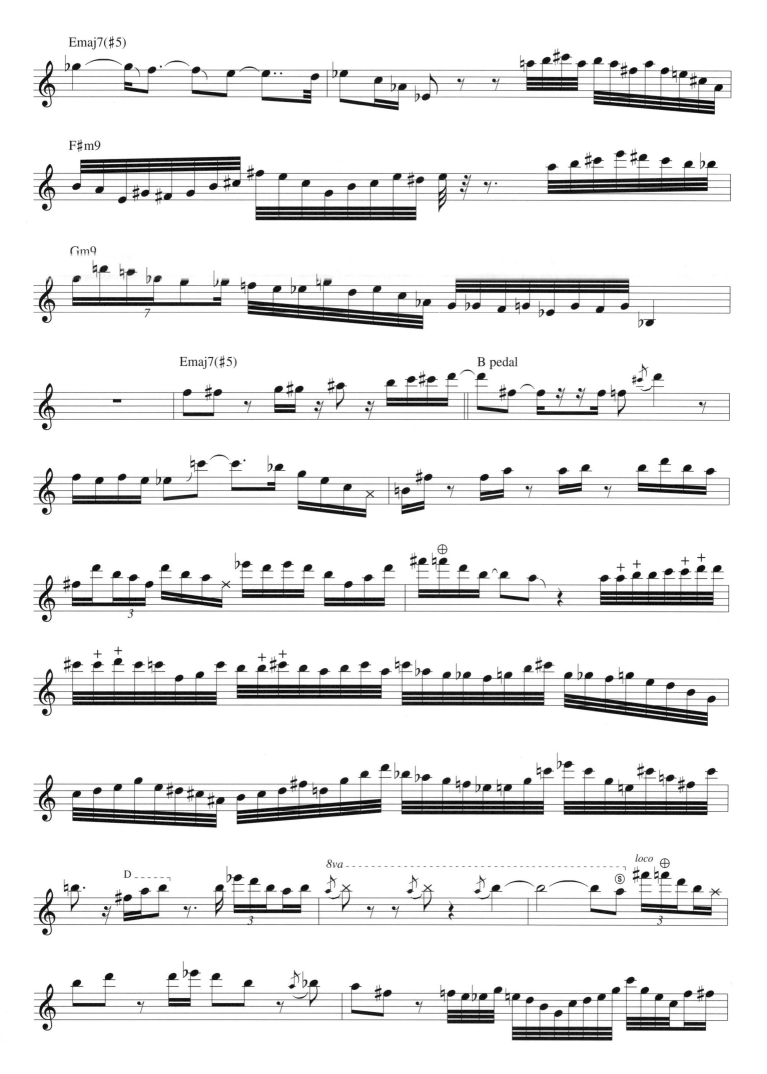

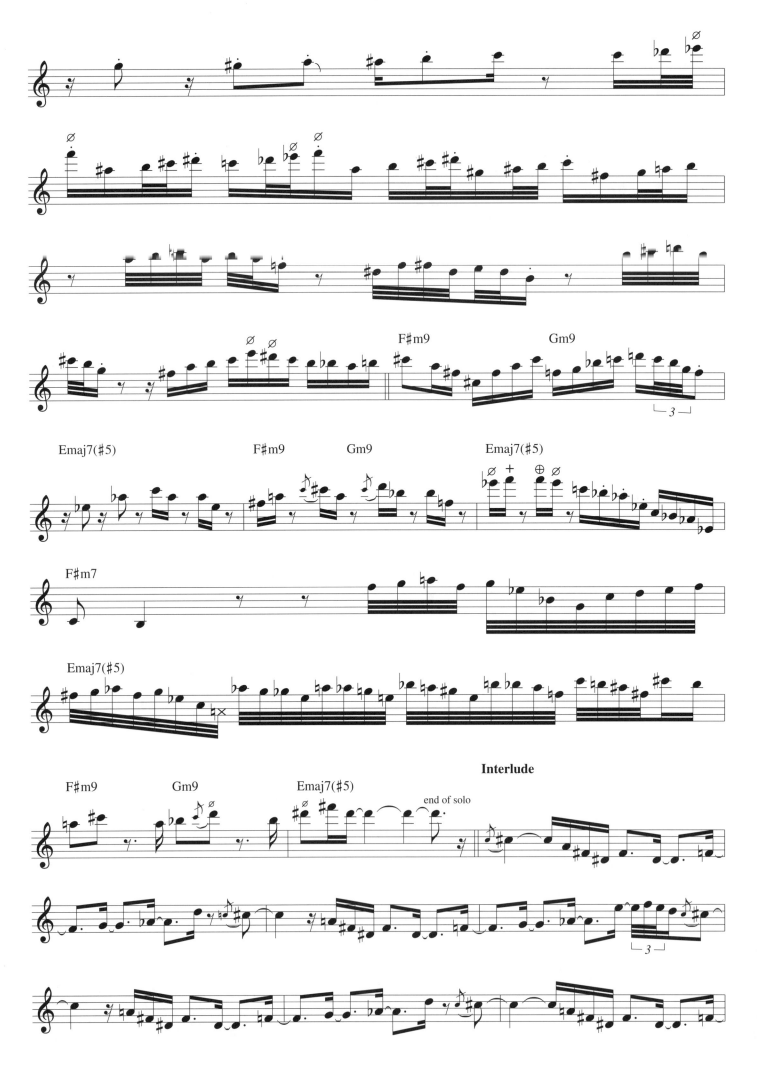

Synth Vibes Solo

Interlude

EWI

Two Blocks from the Edge

from *Two Blocks from the Edge*

By Michael Brecker

Time

Piano Solo

42

ARTIST TRANSCRIPTIONS

Artist Transcriptions are authentic, note-for-note transcriptions of the hottest artists in jazz, pop, and rock today. These outstanding, accurate arrangements are in an easy-to-read format which includes all essential lines. Artist Transcriptions can be used to perform, sequence or reference.

GUITAR & BASS

The Guitar Book of Pierre Bensusan
00699072.................................$19.95

Ron Carter – Acoustic Bass
00672331.................................$16.95

Charley Christian –
The Art of Jazz Guitar
00026704...............................$6.95

Stanley Clarke Collection
00672307.................................$19.95

Larry Coryell – Jazz Guitar Solos
00699140...............................$9.95

Al Di Meola – Cielo E Terra
00604041.................................$14.95

Al Di Meola –
Friday Night in San Francisco
00660115.................................$14.95

Al Di Meola – Music, Words, Pictures
00604043.................................$14.95

Kevin Eubanks Guitar Collection
00672319.................................$19.95

The Jazz Style of Tal Farlow
00673245.................................$19.95

Bela Fleck and the Flecktones
00672359 Melody/Lyrics/Chords....$14.95

David Friesen – Departure
00673221.................................$14.95

David Friesen – Years Through Time
00673253.................................$14.95

Best Of Frank Gambale
00672336.................................$22.95

Jim Hall – Jazz Guitar Environments
00699389 Book/CD....................$19.95

Jim Hall – Exploring Jazz Guitar
00699306.................................$16.95

Scott Henderson Guitar Book
00699330.................................$19.95

Allan Holdsworth –
Reaching for the Uncommon Chord
00604049.................................$14.95

Leo Kottke – Eight Songs
00699215.................................$14.95

Wes Montgomery – Guitar Transcriptions
00675536.................................$14.95

Joe Pass Collection
00672353.................................$14.95

John Patitucci
00673216.................................$14.95

Django Reinhardt Anthology
00027083.................................$14.95

The Genius of Django Reinhardt
00026711.................................$10.95

Django Reinhardt – A Treasury of Songs
00026715.................................$12.95

John Renbourn – The Nine Maidens,
The Hermit, Stefan and John
00699071.................................$12.95

Great Rockabilly Guitar Solos
00692820.................................$14.95

John Scofield – Guitar Transcriptions
00603390.................................$16.95

Andres Segovia –
20 Studies for the Guitar
00006362 Book/Cassette $14.95

Johnny Smith Guitar Solos
00672374.................................$14.95

Mike Stern Guitar Book
00673224.................................$16.95

Mark Whitfield
00672320.................................$19.95

Jack Wilkins – Windows
00673249.................................$14.95

Gary Willis Collection
00672337.................................$19.95

FLUTE

James Newton – Improvising Flute
00660108.................................$14.95

TROMBONE

J.J. Johnson Collection
00672332.................................$19.95

TRUMPET

Randy Brecker
00673234.................................$14.95

The Brecker Brothers...
And All Their Jazz
00672351.................................$19.95

Freddie Hubbard
00673214.................................$14.95

Tom Harrell Jazz Trumpet
00672382.................................$19.95

Jazz Trumpet Solos
00672363...............................$9.95

PIANO & KEYBOARD

Monty Alexander Collection
00672338.................................$19.95

Kenny Barron Collection
00672318.................................$22.95

Warren Bernhardt Collection
00672364.................................$19.95

Billy Childs Collection
00673242.................................$19.95

Chick Corea – Beneath the Mask
00673225.................................$12.95

Chick Corea – Inside Out
00673209.................................$12.95

Chick Corea – Eye of the Beholder
00660007.................................$14.95

Chick Corea – Light Years
00674305.................................$14.95

Chick Corea – Elektric Band
00603126.................................$15.95

Chick Corea – Paint the World
00672300.................................$12.95

Bill Evans Collection
00672365.................................$19.95

Benny Green Collection
00672329.................................$19.95

Don Grolnick Collection
00672396.................................$17.95

Ahmad Jamal Collection
00672322.................................$22.95

Jazz Master Classics for Piano
00672354.................................$14.95

Jelly Roll Morton – The Piano Rolls
00672433.................................$12.95

Michel Petrucciani
00673226.................................$17.95

Bud Powell Classics
00672371.................................$19.95

Joe Sample – Ashes to Ashes
00672310.................................$14.95

Horace Silver Collection
00672303.................................$19.95

Art Tatum Collection
00672316.................................$22.95

Billy Taylor Collection
00672357.................................$24.95

McCoy Tyner
00673215.................................$14.95

SAXOPHONE

Julian "Cannonball" Adderly Collection
00673244.................................$16.95

Michael Brecker
00672337.................................$16.95

Michael Brecker Collection
00672429.................................$17.95

The Brecker Brothers...
And All Their Jazz
00672351.................................$19.95

Benny Carter Plays Standards
00672315.................................$22.95

Benny Carter Collection
00672314.................................$22.95

James Carter Collection
00672394.................................$19.95

John Coltrane – Giant Steps
00672349.................................$19.95

John Coltrane Solos
00673233.................................$22.95

Paul Desmond Collection
00672328.................................$19.95

Stan Getz
00699375.................................$14.95

Stan Getz – Bossa Novas – Saxophone
00672377.................................$16.95

Great Tenor Sax Solos
00673254.................................$18.95

Joe Henderson – Selections from
"Lush Life" & "So Near So Far"
00673252.................................$19.95

Best of Joe Henderson
00672330.................................$22.95

Jazz Master Classics for Tenor Sax
00672350.................................$18.95

Best Of Kenny G
00673239.................................$19.95

Kenny G – Breathless
00673229.................................$19.95

Kenny G – The Moment
00672373.................................$19.95

Joe Lovano Collection
00672326.................................$19.95

James Moody Collection – Sax and Flute
00672372.................................$19.95

The Art Pepper Collection
00672301.................................$19.95

David Sanborn Collection
00675000.................................$14.95

Best of David Sanborn
00120891.................................$14.95

Stanley Turrentine Collection
00672334.................................$19.95

Ernie Watts Saxophone Collection
00673256.................................$18.95

FOR MORE INFORMATION, SEE YOUR LOCAL MUSIC DEALER,
OR WRITE TO:

HAL•LEONARD®
CORPORATION

7777 W. BLUEMOUND RD. P.O. BOX 13819 MILWAUKEE, WI 53213

Visit our web site for a complete listing of our titles with songlists.
www.halleonard.com

Prices and availability subject to change without notice. Some products may not be available outside the U.S.A.   0999